The Cello, How It Works

The Cello, How It Works

A Practical Guide to Cello Ownership

Michael J. Pagliaro

Co-Published in Partnership with the
National Association for Music Education

ROWMAN & LITTLEFIELD
Lanham • Boulder • New York • London

Published by Rowman & Littlefield
An imprint of The Rowman & Littlefield Publishing Group, Inc.
4501 Forbes Boulevard, Suite 200, Lanham, Maryland 20706
www.rowman.com

86-90 Paul Street, London EC2A 4NE, United Kingdom

British Library Cataloguing in Publication Information Available

Library of Congress Cataloging-in-Publication Data

Names: Pagliaro, Michael J., author.
Title: The cello, how it works : a practical guide to cello ownership / Michael J. Pagliaro.
Description: Lanham : Rowman & Littlefield Publishing Group, 2023. | Includes bibliographical references and index. | Summary: "This book will teach you additional information about your instrument that will help you better understand how it works, how to work it, care for it, and how to be a more knowledgeable cellist"— Provided by publisher.
Identifiers: LCCN 2022052752 (print) | LCCN 2022052753 (ebook) | ISBN9781475869125 (paperback) | ISBN 9781475869132 (epub)
Subjects: LCSH: Cello—Maintenance and repair. | Cello—Construction.
Classification: LCC ML910 .P34 2023 (print) | LCC ML910 (ebook) | DDC 787.4/1928—dc23/eng/20221102
LC record available at https://lccn.loc.gov/2022052752
LC ebook record available at https://lccn.loc.gov/2022052753

Table of Contents

Acknowledgments

The following extraordinarily gifted professionals in the field of musical instrument fabrication and distribution have generously granted permission to use information and artwork from their websites. Listed in alphabetical order, they are:

Donna Altieri Bags, info@altieribags.com

bwlibys.blogspot.com, for the picture of a bow hair under a microscope;

Dr. Robin Deverich, for allowing the use of The Advanced Fingering Chart 1st - 7th Positions www.Celloonline.com

Scott Hershey, master luthier at http://www.hersheyviolins.net

Eitan Hoffer, archetier extraordinaire, a specialist in the fabrication of ancient bows at http://www.hoffer-bows.com

Lars Kirmser, publisher and musical instrument specialist at http://www.musictrader.com

Hubert de Launay, info@hubertdelaunay.com

Jenna M. Socci, —B.S. (Psychology), MPS (General Education and Special Education) Thank you for your guidance in establishing a suitable syntax to better communicate with younger students and for your technical assistance with the illustrations.

Christine Patrice Raciti, consultant to the non-fretted string instrument industry. Thank you for your guidance on the details of cello ownership.

Otis A. Tomas, master luthier at www.otis@fiddletree.com

Jimmy Sang Wang, bow manufacturer at http://www.wangbow.com

Introduction

The method book you are now using was written to help you learn how to play the cello. That book contains information on holding your cello, making a sound, reading music, playing different notes, and much more.

This book will teach you additional information about your instrument that will help you better understand how it works, how to work it, care for it, and how to be a more knowledgeable cellist.

The first section reviews information that might be on the first few pages of your method book. Even if you know that information, spend a few moments reading this section to see if you can find something you did not yet learn. From there on, you will learn information that not many students will ever know.

You do not have to read this book in the order in which the chapters appear. Start at any chapter that may interest you, and then, as you progress, move around to the chapters related to your cello studies.

NOTE: In the music world, the terms tailpiece, pegbox, chinrest, and soundpost can also be written as two words. You might see them as tail piece, peg box, chin rest, and sound post.

Note: The following explains a system used throughout all music studies called *Scientific Pitch Notation*. This is a valuable tool that can serve you throughout your music career.

Scientific Pitch Notation helps you know exactly where a note is located on the staff without seeing the note in print. This system uses a combination of letters and numerals (alphanumeric) to tell you where a note is in the entire range of notes. An example would be middle C, whose alphanumeric name is C4. The C one octave below middle C is C3. The C one octave above middle C is C5. The notes going up between these Cs keep the C's numeral until the next C is reached. Examples would be C4, D4, E4, F4, G4, A4, B4, C5, D5, etc. The figure below shows the alphanumeric symbol for all notes.

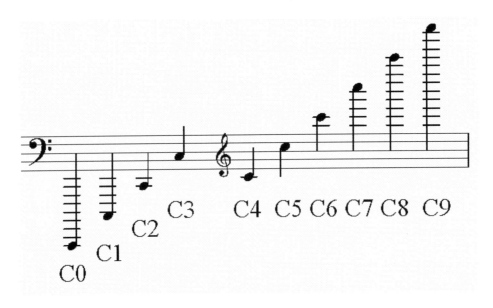

Chapter 1

What Are the Parts of My Cello and How Do They Work?

Lesson One

Cello Parts

Let's begin by learning the names of some parts of your cello. Using the picture below as a guide, locate the named parts on your own cello.

A. scroll
B. pegbox
C. pegs
D. neck
E. fingerboard
F. bridge
G. end pin screw
H. tailpiece
I. end pin
J. tailgut
K. top
L. "ƒ" hole
M. side
N. back
O. purfling

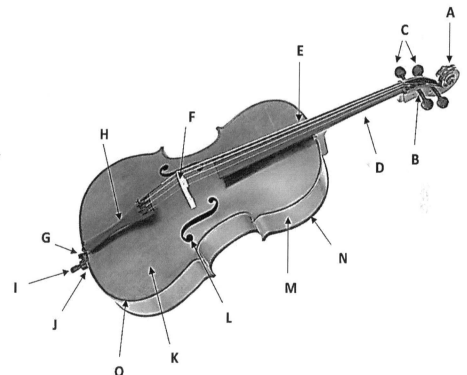

Next are the names of the parts that support the strings and produce sounds.

1. strings
2. bridge
3. top
4. sound post (inside)
5. back
6. bass bar (inside top)
7. sides
8. "*f*" hole
9. purfling

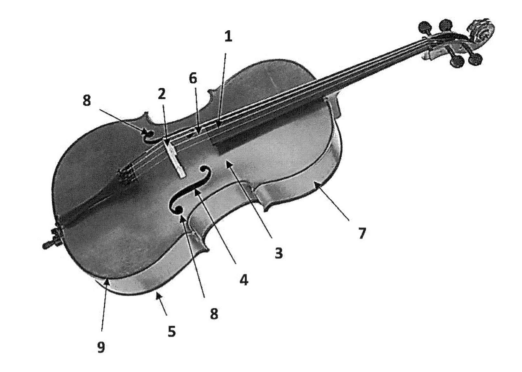

Let's look inside a cello.

Supporting the top and back of your cello are the:

A. ribs and linings
B. top and bottom block
C. corner blocks
D. bass bar
E. sound post

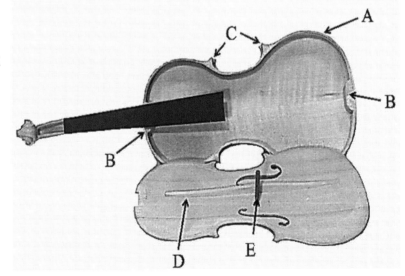

All the inside parts work together to strengthen the sound you hear as you bow or pluck a string.

Lesson Two

How Do These Parts Work?

The Bridge — The sound you produce when you pluck or bow a string travels to the feet of the bridge and then to the top of your cello.

"f" **Holes** — *"f"* holes are the f-shaped holes cut into the top of your cello. There is one *"f"* hole on each side of the bridge. These *"f"* shaped openings let out the sound that is vibrating inside the body of your cello.

The Sound Post— The sound post is inside the body of your cello. Look inside through the *"f"* hole on the A string side. The sound post is made of soft wood. It supports the top of your cello and sends the sound of the high notes from the top of the instrument to its back.

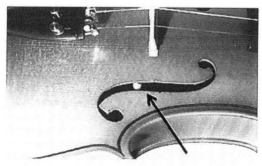

The Bass Bar —The bass bar is on the underside of the top of your cello beneath the bridge foot on the C string side. The bass bar strengthens the cello's top while carrying the lower notes throughout the instrument's top. You can see a bass bar by placing a dentist's mirror in the *"f"* hole on the C string side of your instrument.

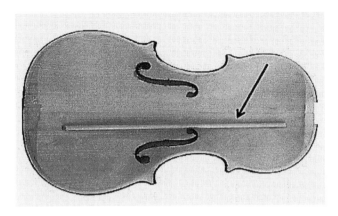

The combination of the bridge, sound post, and bass bar with your cello's top and back produces the sound you hear when you bow or pluck a string.

The Sides and Back — The sides and back of your cello hold the instrument together.

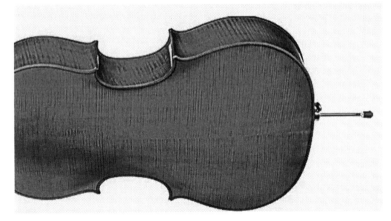

These parts are made of very strong maple wood. The strength is needed to support the pressure the tightened strings put on the cello's top. When all four strings are tuned, the pressure they put on the instrument equals about 85 pounds, the weight of a pile of almost 52 iPads.

Purfling — Two parallel strips of ebony, a dark hard wood, are inserted into the surface around the edge of the top and back of your cello.

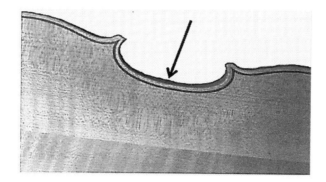

These two strips of wood are called purfling. They outline the area that will vibrate on the top and back of the cello. They also add strength to the edges of the instrument's body.

Lesson Three

The Sound Voyage

Using the same picture where you learned the names of your cello's parts, let's follow the trip sound makes throughout your cello as you play.

When you bow or pluck a string (1).

its motion (vibration) is picked up by the bridge (2).

and sent to the top of the cello (3).

That vibration travels to the sound post inside the cello(4).

which then carries the vibration to the cello's back (5).

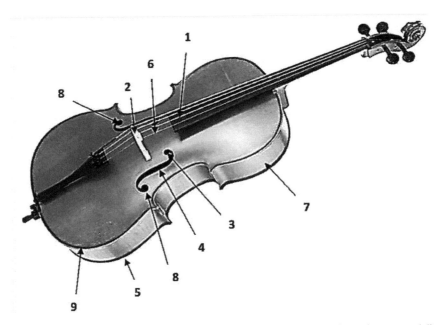

and is spread throughout the cello's top by the bass bar under the top (6).

The top and back of the cello are supported by its sides (7).

The motion of all these parts sets the air inside the cello's body into a pumping action that forces the sound out through the *"f"* holes (8).

The small wooden strips called purfling (9) around the edge of the cello control the vibration of sound throughout the top and back and give strength to the edges.

Lesson Four

Tuning Your Cello

Tuning your cello will be easy if you understand how the pegs and fine tuners work.

The cello has wedge-shaped (narrower at one end than the other) wooden pegs, which are forced into holes in the pegbox.

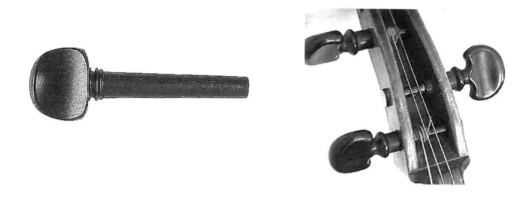

The term pitch refers to how high or low a note is. To tune your cello, you must hear the correct pitch for each string. The open strings on a cello are pictured below.

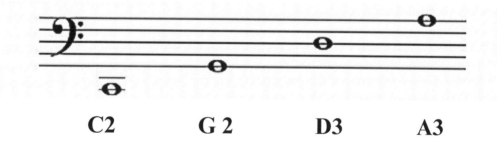

C2   G 2   D3   A3

You can get the right sounds for C, G, D, and A from a piano, a pitch pipe, or an electronic tuner. These are just some of the many different tuning aids you can use. Below are a piano keyboard, two pitch pipes, and an electronic tuner. (See chapter 4 on cello accessories for more information on these devices).

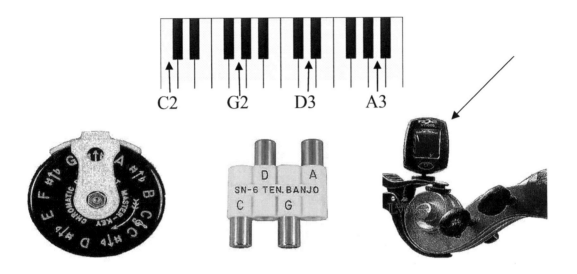

You can also search *YouTube tuning a cello,* where several videos will help you do a perfect job of tuning your cello.

The following is one of the recommended ways to tune your cello.

1. Hold the instrument with the endpin on the floor and the strings facing you.

2. Select the pitch you need (C, G, D, or A) for the string you are tuning.

3. Sound the pitch of the string you are tuning on the tuning device and try to fix that sound in your mind. Singing the pitch with the tuner will help.

4. When you have the pitch firmly fixed in your mind, pluck the string to be tuned.

The next step is very important to successful tuning.

5. While the string is sounding the note you have just plucked, _slowly_ tighten the string by turning the peg toward the top of the scroll. As you turn the peg, _push it in_ so that it is forced into the holes of the pegbox.

6. This picture shows how to turn and push in the peg as you tune. It is very important that you force the pegs into the peg holes. If you just turn the peg, it will not hold the string in tune.

7. While you are slowly turning and pushing the peg in, continue to pluck the string, listening to the sound get higher. When it reaches the pitch you have in mind, stop. The string will be tuned.

8. If you need to adjust the pitch just a tiny bit more, you can do so using the fine tuner on the tailpiece to raise or lower the pitch in small amounts.

9. With the front of the instrument facing you, pluck the string again while you turn the fine tuner to the right to raise the pitch or to the left to lower the pitch.

10. When you have tuned the four strings, check them again, starting with the A string. Sometimes the tuning process will slightly change the pitch of the strings you have already tuned.

11. Finely, play each open string with your bow and check the pitch for correctness.

Lesson Five

Your Bow

The Bow — The cello bow is easily identified by the rounded back of the frog (arrow).

Using your method book, with your teacher's help, you learned how to hold and use a bow. Now let's learn about the parts of a bow and how it makes the sounds you are playing.

Bow Hair — A cello bow is made up of about 195 hairs connected to a stick. The hair used on cello bows can be taken from a horse's tail or can be manmade. Horsehair is the better choice, but some very good manmade (synthetic) bow hair is in use.

Looking closely at bow hair, you will think it is smooth. But look at bow hair under a microscope, and you will be surprised to see that the surface is rough. The picture below shows magnified horsehair.

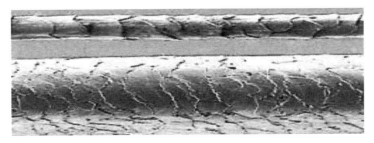

Bow Hair under a Microscope
Courtesy of bwlibys.blogspot.com

It is this rough surface, along with cello rosin, that you apply to the hair that catches on to a string causing it to vibrate and make a sound.

Bow Parts — The diagram below shows how the hair is connected to the bow stick.

The end of the bow hair (A) is wedged tightly into a box-shaped cutout called a mortise (B) at the tip of the bow.

The hair is held in place by a wooden, wedge-shaped plug (C) that is cut to exactly fit the space in the cutout box.

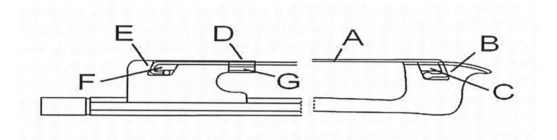

A metal band called a ferrule (D) is placed over the hair, which is carefully drawn along the bow, tied at the end, and forced into another box-shaped cutout in the frog. (E).

Another wooden wedge-shaped plug is placed into the box (F) to keep the hair in place.

Finally, a slide and a third wooden wedge are placed between the ferrule and the frog (G) to help spread the hairs and keep them in place.

Tightening and Loosening Bow Hair — You probably learned how to tighten and loosen your bow at your first lesson. Let's take a closer look at the bow parts we use when we adjust our bow hair.

This is the frog end of a cello bow.

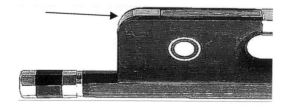

Below is a picture of the eyelet, the screw that fits into the eyelet, and a frog with the screw and eyelet together.

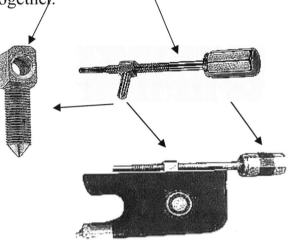

When you turn the screw, it moves in or out of the eyelet, which is attached to the frog. The eyelet pulls or pushes the frog back and forth. Turning the screw to the right will pull the frog back and tighten the bow hair. Turning the screw to the left will push the frog forward and loosen the bow hair.

Lesson Six

Changing Notes

The cello has four strings that are tuned to C, G, D, and A. You can raise the pitch of each string by pressing the string to the fingerboard with the fingers of your left hand, as pictured.

This is how it works:

As you press a finger on the string, you shorten the vibrating part of the string. When plucked or bowed, shorter strings produce higher sounds. You learned in your lesson book how to finger the different notes starting with the first finger about two and a half inches down from the nut on any string. That is called first position. To be sure you have your finger in the right spot, set your tuning device to that note and check the pitch.

There are seven playing positions on the cello. The following charts are reproduced with permission of Dr. Robin Deverich from his celloonline.com website.

Note: On the staff in the sixth and Seventh positions, you will see this symbol called a movable C clef. It makes that line middle C4. All the surrounding lines and spaces follow up or down with the usual letter names. The C clef is used to avoid the use of lines above the staff (ledger lines), making reading those notes easier.

Dr. Robin Deverich, the creator of the website www.celloonline, has consented to include the Advanced Fingering Chart 1st - 7th Positions.

Using this chart as your guide, you will see that you are playing in:

1. first position when your first finger is one whole step up from the open string.

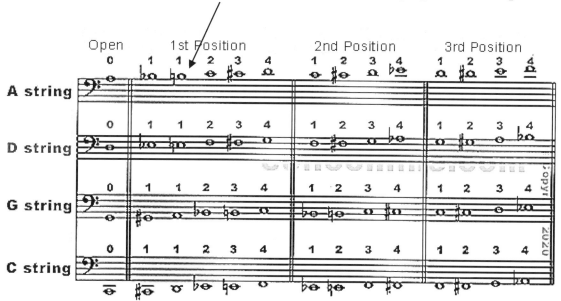

2. second position when your first finger is where your second finger was in first
position.

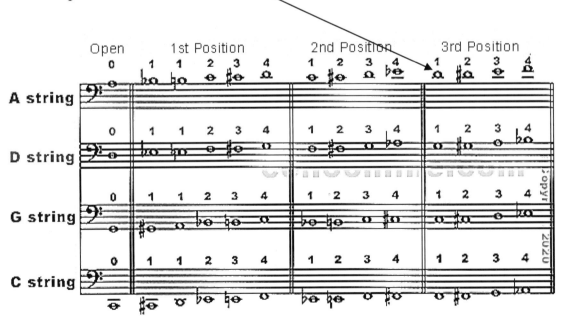

3. third position when your first finger is where your fourth finger was in
first position.

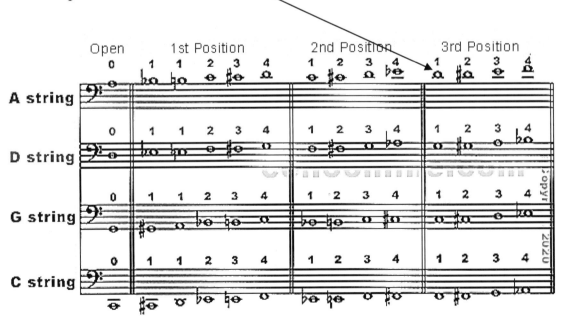

14

4. fourth position when your first finger is where your third finger was in
   third position.

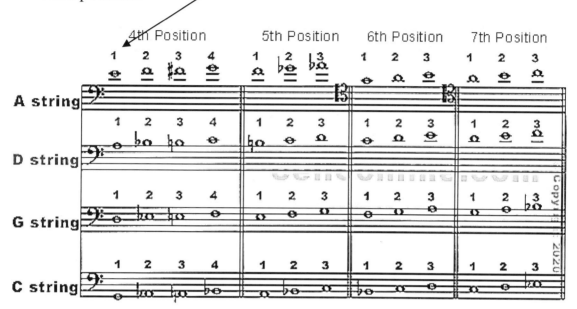

5. fifth position, when your first finger is where your second finger was in
fourth position.

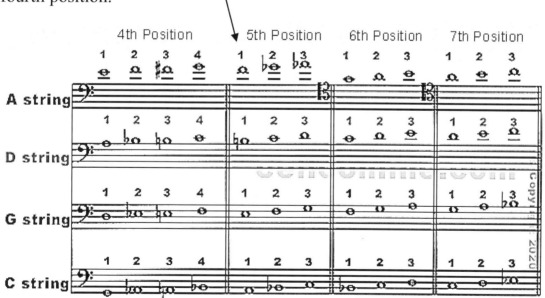

6. sixth position when your first finger is where your forth finger was in fourth position.

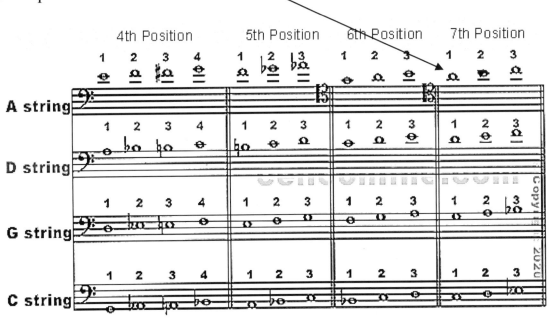

7. seventh position when your first finger is where your second finger was in sixth position.

Position Charts Compliments of celloonline.com

The following is a basic fingering chart for the notes on a cello.

To finger a note, press the string at the position noted by the dots on the finger-board chart.

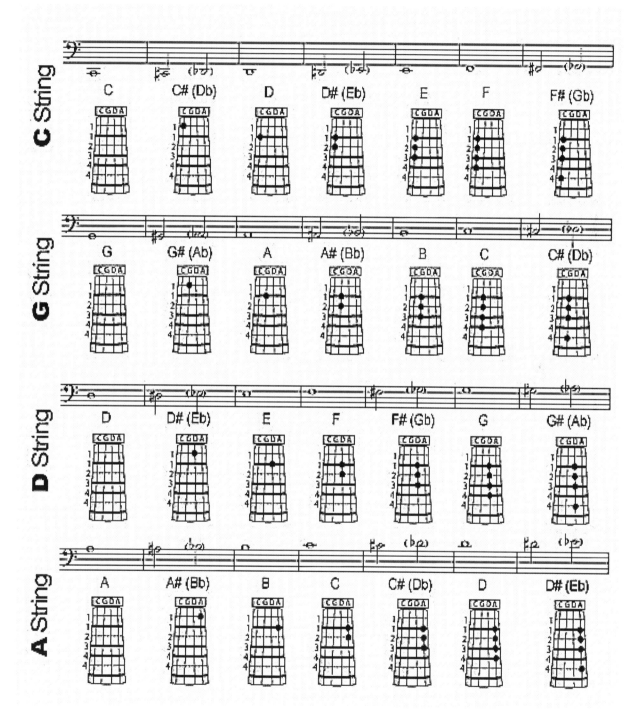

Fingering Chart Complements of Celloonline.com

NOTES

Chapter 2

How Do I Care for My Cello Outfit?

Your cello and bow need very special care because:

1. they are made of wood that can crack or break if dropped or treated roughly.

2. the wood can be damaged by extreme heat, cold, or very damp or dry air.

3. the wood has a fine finish that can be scratched or damaged by dirt and rosin dust.

Lesson One

Let's see how we can prevent these mishaps

1. To avoid damage from dropping your cello, always place it on a safe flat surface or in its case. Do not leave it resting against a chair.

2. Never put music or other books in your hard cello case. The case is made to fit the shape of your cello and does not have extra space for other items. Soft cases usually have a pocket on the back for extra items and one in the front for the bow.

3. Store your cello in your house where you would be comfortable, not in the attic, basement, or garage. If your cello is in its case and in your way, put it in a closet.

4. Never put your cello in the trunk of a car. Keep it in the car with you, where the temperature is comfortable. But! Never leave the cello in an unoccupied car. The cello can become too hot or cold and be stolen.

5. The finish on your cello is probably varnish or some form of lacquer. Extra items, in your case, can scratch these finishes. Always keep your rosin, tuner, and other small items in the pocket on the back of your soft case and the bow in the bow pocket on the front of your case. Hard cases will have various pockets and compartments for accessories inside the case.

6. Wash your hands before you handle your cello. Natural hand oil or other substances on your hands can damage the surface of your instrument.

7. Follow the instruction in lesson 2 on wiping the surfaces of your instrument and strings after each use. Rosin dust left on these surfaces can damage them.

8. When traveling with your cello, keep the instrument in the same location you occupy. A bus, train, or plane's luggage compartment is not acceptable for storage during travel. Keep the instrument as close to you as possible.

Lesson Two

Keeping Your Cello Outfit Clean and Properly Adjusted

After each use:

1. Wipe the surfaces of the instrument and the strings with a soft cotton cloth to remove any rosin dust, natural skin oils, and perspiration.

2. Wipe the bow stick and frog with the same cloth.

3. If your cello or bow stick show signs of dirt or rosin that will not come off with the dry cloth, it is time to use cello polish, which can be bought in any music store or online. Ask your teacher what he or she uses for the same problem. Be careful not to get polish on the bow hair.

Making Minor Adjustments

Adjusting the Bridge

(Ask your teacher to help you the first time you try this.)

Each time you tune your cello, the strings move the bridge a tiny bit toward the fingerboard. To adjust your bridge:

1. Loosen the strings just a bit.

2. Place the instrument in playing position.

3. Lean over the cello and, using your thumb and forefinger of each hand, grip the bridge on the middle of each side and move it back to its upright position.

4. The bridge feet should be in complete contact with the instrument's top.

5. Re-tune the instrument (chapter 1, lesson 4).

Bridge Placement

The exact position of the bridge on your cello is very important because the bridge carries the string's sound down to the cello's top and then throughout the entire instrument.

To check your bridge's location — Look at the middle of your *"f"* holes, and you will see a notch on each side. The bridge feet should be in line with the notches on the bridge side of the *"f"* holes.

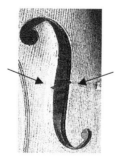

Lesson Three

Sticking and Slipping Pegs

You learned in chapter 1 that the cello has wedge-shaped wooden pegs that are forced into holes in the pegbox.

There are times when your cello pegs will either slip or get stuck. Usually, they will slip in the winter when the air is cold and dry, and they will stick in the summer when the weather is hot and humid. This happens because wood will shrink in cold-dry weather and swell in hot, humid weather.

Pegs and pegboxes are made of different kinds of wood. When the two kinds of wood shrink or swell, they do so at different rates, so the shrinking pegs and peg holes will loosen and slip, and the swelling pegs and peg holes will tighten up and stick.

Treating Peg Problems

1. Check to see if the hole drilled in the peg to receive a string is at the narrowend of the peg.

2. Starting from that point with the string in the hole, wind the string around the peg two turns toward the small end of the peg.

3. Then, guide the string across and over the hole toward the larger side of the peg and complete the turning.

4. The strings should be lined up against one another. There should be no string buildup against the pegbox wall. If the hole is too close to the pegbox, it should be relocated by a luthier.

To treat slipping pegs:

1. The old-fashioned way was to remove the pegs and apply chalk or soap to them at the points of contact where the peg meets the pegbox.

2. A newer way is to remove the pegs and apply peg compound to them. Peg compound is a paste that you can buy in any music store. Follow the directions on the package.

3. The newest, easiest, and best way is to apply Peg Drops as instructed on the package. With this product, there is no need to remove the pegs.

Lesson Four

Caring for Your Fine Tuners

Each time you turn the knob on your fine tuner to the right, the bottom bar gets lower. When it reaches the bottom, turn it back to its original position and re-tune your cello.

Lesson Five

Bow Care

1. Always keep your bow where you keep your cello. They are safest in their case.

2. Do not leave your bow on a music stand or a chair. The bow can easily be knocked off the stand or be sat upon if it is on a chair.

3. When preparing to use your bow, tighten your bow hair to the point where you can fit your index finger in the space between the bow stick and bow hair, and then further adjust the hair if necessary.

4. When your bow hair is tight, your bow stick should curve toward the hair. If it is not curved, show it to your teacher for advice.

5. When not in use, loosen the hair on your bow.

6. Never touch the bow hair with your fingers. The natural oil from your skin will soil the hairs, and the bow will not work well.

7. If a hair breaks, do not pull it off the bow. Cut it off at the frog and tip with scissors to avoid damage to the other hairs.

Cleaning Your Bow Hair

1. To clean your bow hair, moisten a soft cloth with rubbing alcohol. With that cloth, wipe the hair in an up-and-down motion until it is clean. Do not let the alcohol touch the bow stick because the alcohol will damage the finish on the wood.

2. When the alcohol on the hair dries, gently run a comb up and down the hairs to loosen them. Then rosin your bow as usual. Ask your teacher about a product called the "Bow Hair Rejuvenation Kit" (p. 35), which is excellent for keeping your bow in playing condition.

3. When a bow is left in a case for a long time, you may find that the hairs are falling off the stick. This is caused by tiny insects called dermestids (bow bugs). If this happens, remove the bow from the case, cut off all the bow hair with a scissor, discard the hair and send the bow to a bow maker for rehairing.

4. Next, vacuum the case thoroughly, giving special care to the corners and edges. Then spray the case with an insecticide, and let the case remain open in a bright sunlit place for a few days.

Cleaning Your Bow Stick — After each use, use a soft cloth to wipe the rosin dust from your bow stick. If your bow stick is caked with dry rosin, use a cello polish to clean the stick. Be extra careful not to get any cello polish on the bow hair.

Lesson Six

Case Care

Cleaning Your Cello Case — Keeping the inside and outside of your cello case clean is important. The insides of hard cello cases are lined with a special kind of material that will protect the cello from damage. That material collects lint, rosin dust, and any other small matter that enters your case.

To care for the inside of your case, use a vacuum with a hose and pointed nozzle or a hand vac and go at it. Be sure to get into all the corners and seams in the case.

The outside of hard cello cases can be made of plastic or a hard material covered with fabric. Molded plastic cases can be wiped with a damp cloth and, when dry, polished with a spray polish like Pledge. Fabric-covered case cleaning depends on the fabric. Usually, this is canvas and can be wiped with a damp cloth (no soap) to remove any dirt or dust that has collected on the case cover. Cello soft cases can also be vacuumed inside and wiped clean on the outside with a damp cloth.

Cellos and bows can last hundreds of years if properly cared for. The process is not hard to do, nor does it take much time. Make a habit of regularly going through the above-listed procedures, and your cello might also be here a few hundred years from now.

Lesson Seven

Adjustments

Strings — The strings on your cello rest on the cello's nut (A), bridge (B), and tail-piece (C) (see arrows). Over time, these three areas can wear down. If you see string wear or wear on the slots where the string meets the nut, bridge, or tailpiece, ask your teacher's advice on how to deal with the problem.

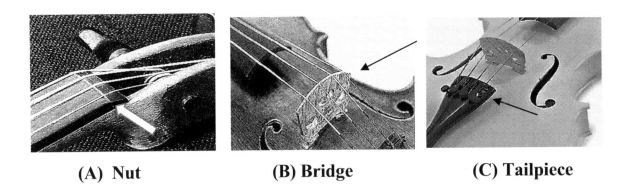

(A) Nut   (B) Bridge   (C) Tailpiece

If the string is wearing out, simply replace it. If one of the three parts shows wear, you will need a luthier (cello maker) to replace the nut and the bridge. You can replace the tailpiece with your teacher's help.

Summary — Properly caring for your cello, bow, and case will give the outfit a long life and allow it to serve you in the best way possible. These are the tools that you will use to make music. A good student with good equipment will make good music.

Chapter 3

How Should I Plan My Practice Sessions?

I'm sure you have heard that "practice makes perfect." Well, practice can make perfect, but only if you practice with understanding, patience, and the will to "get it right." Playing an exercise or musical selection many times over will not make it better unless you understand how the piece should sound and know what to do to make it sound that way. Playing a piece incorrectly over and over can result in your learning to play it wrong really well.

The following are some suggestions that will help you get the best results from your cello practice period:

1. Select a place in your home where you can practice without disturbing your family and where their daily life will not distract you from your work.

2. Pick a practice time that comfortably fits your daily study schedule. Try to use that same time each day for your cello studies.

3. Set a long-term general goal. In what way do you want to improve your playing? Think of bowing, playing in tune, phrasing, dexterity (moving your fingers fast), and making beautiful music beautifully.

4. Have a plan for each practice period. What part of your long-term goal do you want to accomplish in each period?

5. How long and how often should you practice? Daily practice is the best road to success. However, the amount of time you practice should vary with your short-term goal. Shorter daily practice periods produce better results than less frequent long sessions.

6. After you have planned your goal and begun to practice, decide on the amount of time and how often practice will be necessary to achieve each target.

7. Discuss your plans with your teacher, who will be able to help you make the plan and reach your goal. The amount of time you spend practicing is not as important as what you accomplish during your practice period.

8. Equipment – It is important that you have all the equipment necessary to have a successful practice period. Your equipment should include a music stand, metronome, pitch pipe, comfortable chair, rock stop, rosin, cleaning cloth, tuning device, and anything else you feel you need to be comfortable.

The Process

1. Begin your practice period with a careful tuning of your cello. Use whatever apps or tuning devices you feel will be best for you.

2. Warm up, starting with simple scales in first position using quarter notes. Play slowly and listen. Are you playing in tune?

3. After you are sure that you have the quarter note scales down, add rhythmic patterns of your own creation to those same scales. Listen carefully to intonation as you play. Playing in tune is a must.

4. As you advance, you can expand the warmup material to include exercises and any other music you enjoy playing.

5. Follow your warmup by playing a tune that you like. Enjoy the music.

6. Improvisation is fun. Make up your own tune or try to play a tune "by ear." No need for printed music here.

7. Now, start practicing the material your teacher assigned in your last lesson. Follow the instructions carefully. Listen to yourself, sing the music before you play it, be sure you are playing in tune, and feel the rhythm.

8. Record yourself on your mobile phone as you play. Then listen to the recording and be very critical of your intonation, phrasing, and general musicianship.

9. Did you like what you heard? If your answer is yes – great! If it is not, think of what you did not like and figure out how you can make it better. Then, make it better.

10. Check again to ensure you are playing in tune, using proper phrasing and bowing. Are you keeping a proper playing position?

Apps and Your Mobile Phone

Using your mobile phone or computer, you can search for "apps for cello practice and tuning." You will find many free ones that will help you tune and practice better. Some sites also have free music that you can print. Others show playing techniques and play-a-long sessions where you join others to play cello music. Use the same search on YouTube, and you will find many sites you will enjoy watching while learning about playing your cello.

String Ovation site contains a wide variety of cello apps, including tuning, sight-reading, music theory, ear training, intonation, and much more. The world of the cello is just a few clicks away.

NOTES

Chapter 4

What Items (Accessories) Will I Need to Help Me Play My Cello?

An accessory is something that will help you use your cello but that is not part of a basic cello outfit. The descriptions and pictures of accessories below are just some of these items. You can find hundreds more online.

Rosin — Rosin, made from tree sap (resin), is used to make the hair on your cello bow sticky. This makes the hair grip the cello string as you bow to produce sound.

Rosin comes in shades of amber (yellow), from light to dark. Prices range from 99 cents to $35. and in some "very special" cases, even more. If you are a beginning student, starting with the least expensive rosin available would be best. It will work fine until your teacher recommends a change or you feel you need something different. Be sure to use "cello rosin," as it is specially made for your cello bow.

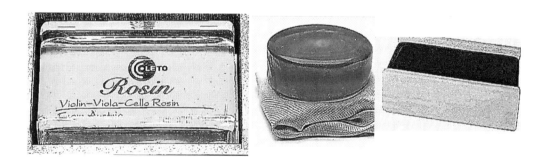

Rosin can have different degrees of hardness and color. Hard rosin, usually light amber, gives a dry powdery result. Its gripping power is lighter and usually best for the cello. Soft rosin, darker in color, has a stickier texture and provides increased gripping power for the bow hair. This greater gripping power will produce a stronger sound.

Tuning Forks — The tuning fork is the most basic device used to hear a pitch. Tuning forks are U-shaped and made of metal with a handle at the base of the U.

Hold a tuning fork by the handle and strike the tines (prongs) on a hard surface. The tines will vibrate. Then touch the stem to a hard surface, and you will hear the tone (pitch) produced by the vibrations. You can get a tuning fork for any pitch, but A440 (440 vibrations per second) is the pitch A you would use to tune your cello A string.

Pitch Pipes — Pitch pipes are a necessary accessory for any cello player. The simplest pitch pipe is made with four small pipes joined together. Each pipe is tuned to match the pitch of one string on the cello. The pitches from low to high for the cello are C, G, D, and A. You blow gently into the correct pipe to hear the pitch you need to tune a string. The picture on the right shows a pitch pipe with the four notes of the cello and tenor banjo open strings.

A chromatic pitch pipe is round and has a marked opening for every pitch, including the scale's sharps and flats (chromatics). The notes start at C and progress in half steps up to the next C in the scale. You can pick any note, slide the white marker to that note's position on the pitch pipe, blow into that hole, and hear your chosen pitch.

Electronic Tuners — There are several kinds of electronic tuners. The simpler type produces the four pitches of the open strings for your cello. Other models have a full chromatic scale from which you select the pitch needed. Press the correct button, and you will hear the pitch.

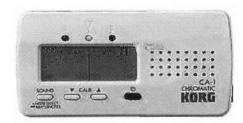

A more advanced type of tuner has a screen which shows an image of the pitch being sounded. When you bow or pluck an open string, a needle on a screen will tell you if the sound is up (sharp), down (flat), or spot-on the pitch you want. You can then tune the string up or down until the correct pitch is reached.

Clip-on tuners — These are very convenient because you can read the results as you play a note. Below is pictured only one of many available in position on a bridge.

Apps or Applications — Apps and websites on tuning can be found on your mobile phone, iPad, and computer. If you use one of these, try not to be distracted by using your practice time to try the technology. Amazon.com shows five pages, each with about fifteen different tuners for a total of seventy-five tuners now on the market.

Fine Tuners — Fine tuners are attached to the tailpiece or a cello string and are available in different forms. The Suzuki model fine tuners are independent tuners that are attached directly to a string.

 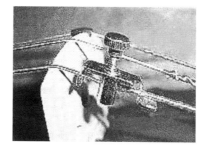

Another style of fine tuner attaches to the tailpiece, and the string is then connected directly to the fine tuner.

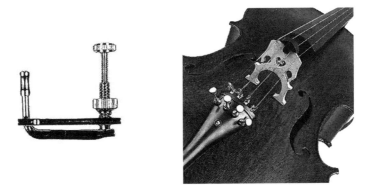

There are also tuners that are part of the tailpiece. The string is attached to the fine tuner instead of directly to the tailpiece.

Peg Treatment — As you read on page 22, Slipping and stuck pegs are an everyday problem for cellists. Since the pegbox and the pegs are made of different kinds of wood, they expand and contract at different rates, and the pegs can either slip or stick.

The oldest cure for this problem is peg compound, a heavy paste that you put on the pegs to stop them from sticking or slipping. You must remove the string from the peg, remove the peg, apply the compound to the peg, work the peg back into the peg hole, and then replace the string into the hole in the peg. Not an easy job.

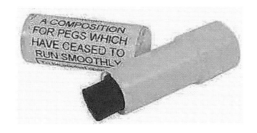

An easier solution to peg problems that works well is ***Peg Drops***. You loosen the peg with the string in place, put one drop on the peg at the two points where it comes in contact with the pegbox, and then slide the peg back into place.

Bow Hair Rejuvenation Kit — To remove rosin buildup and dirt from handling and the environment, use the ***Bow Hair Rejuvenation Kit***. In the kit, you will find a liquid bow-cleaning solvent, a cloth with which to apply the solvent, a comb to straighten out the hairs after the solvent dries, and a liquid rosin solution to apply to the hair at the end of the cleaning process. Follow the instructions. It works.

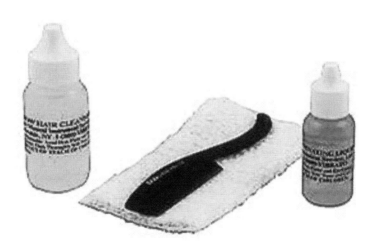

Rock Stop — AKA endpin stopper, endpin anchor rest holder, or cello floor protector is a device used to prevent cello endpins from slipping. Below is pictured a

Wolf Super Endpin Stop   **Rock Stop**   **End Pin Anchor**

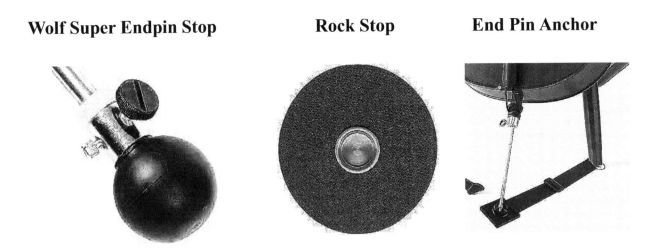

There are many more.

    Strings — As you progress in your studies, you will want to learn more about the different kinds of cello strings and how they can improve the sound of your cello. A computer search shows fifty-seven different brands of cello strings. These strings can be made of gut, steel, perlon (plastic fiber), nylon, silk, chromium/steel, silver, and gold. Each type of string produces a different sound and can change the tone quality of your cello.

    Steel or Steel Core strings are the strongest, produce the brightest sound, stay in tune longer, and are best for use by beginning players.

    Gut strings produce a more mellow sound, but they react to changes in temperature and humidity, causing problems with keeping your cello in tune. Gut strings tend to break more easily than steel strings.

    Gut Core strings are gut strings that are wound with silver or aluminum. These produce a fuller sound and are stronger than plain gut.

    Synthetic Core strings are made with nylon or other manmade material as a core. These strings are stronger than gut, do not react greatly to temperature and humidity changes, and stay in tune longer.

Strings are made with a ball, loop, or knot end to connect to the tailpiece. The loop and ball ends are usually found on most strings, whereas the knot end is used for gut strings without windings.

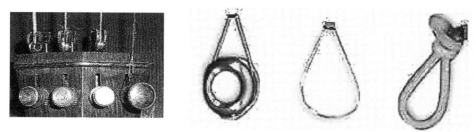

Mutes — A mute changes the tone, quality, and volume of a cello's sound. Mutes can be made of wood with three prongs, a rubber disc, wire with a plastic arch, or five rubber prongs. Below are four examples of mutes for a cello.

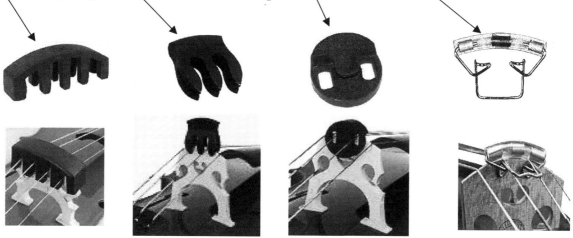

Wolf Tone Eliminator — A wolf tone is a howling-like sound that can occur on some cellos when playing certain notes (usually in the area of G). Placing a wolf tone eliminator on the offending string below the bridge will eliminate that sound. Below are pictured two of the most popular types of wolf tone eliminators.

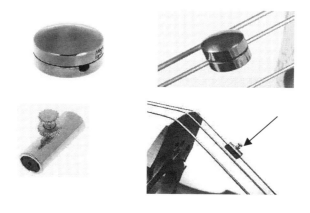

Cello Stands— Between use, it is best to have your cello on a stand instead of on its side on the floor, which could damage the edges of the instrument. Below are pictured three different kinds of stands. Each positions the instrument differently. There are many variations of those types.

Cello Cases — Cello cases made of fabric, usually canvas, are called soft cases or gig bags. Hard cases are usually made of some form of plastic with a felt inside coating. Others are available with a padded lining to offer greater protection for your cello.

A basic gig bag will have a simple carrying strap on its side, a pocket for the bow on the front, and an accessories pocket on the back. The three examples below show a basic bag, one with wheels and one with multiple carrying straps.

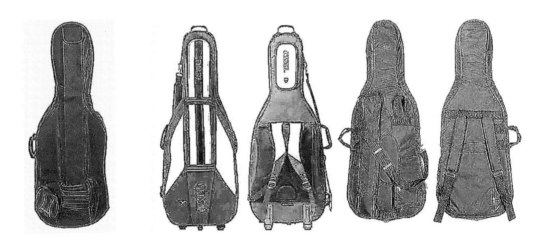

Hard cases can be made of carbon fiber, plastic, or wood covered with canvas or other fabric. These cases are heavier to carry but offer greater protection for your cello. Hard cases also come with wheels and multiple carrying straps. Below is a picture of carbon fiber, Polypropylene, and wood covered with canvas cases.

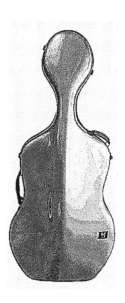

Another type of hard cello case, called a suspension case, has a series of padded shelves and Velcro straps that keep the instrument's body from being in direct contact with the back of the case. The instrument is suspended inside the case.

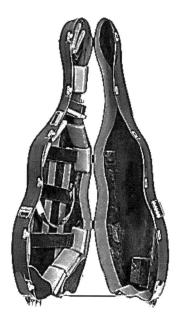

Bow Cases — If you use a soft cello bag for storage and travel, your bow will be in a pocket, usually in the front of the bag. That bow storage offers little protection. A safe way for bow storage and transportation is a bow case, as pictured below. Note the accessory bag on the front cover.

Hygrometers — A hygrometer measures the level of humidity in a cello case. If a hygrometer shows a dry climate, you will need to place a humidifier in the case. Below are two of the many designs of hygrometers.

Digital

Analog

Humidifiers — A Dampit humidifier is a perforated rubber tube filled with an absorbent material that holds water. When your cello is not in use, insert the Dampit tube soaked in water into the instrument's body through the *"f"* hole. Remove the Dampit when you use the instrument. A humidity-measuring color chart is included with the Dampit kit.

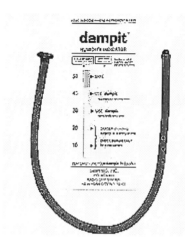

Search "cello case humidifiers" on Google Images, and you will find more of these products.

Music Stands — Music stands are made in three designs. There are stands that fold, those that are rigid or non-folding, and tabletop stands.

A folding stand or sheet music stand is very useful for a beginning student. It is lightweight, totally portable, and very inexpensive. Folding stands can also be purchased with a carrying case for even more convenient portability. These stands can easily be knocked over, and the lightweight parts can be bent out of shape.

A rigid design stand, sometimes called a concert, stage, or orchestra music stand, is not easy to carry, is quite heavy, and is made to be used in one place. They are more expensive than folding stands but are very stable, able to hold a large amount of music, and are very strong. These stands can cost two to four times that of a folding stand.

A small tabletop stand does not have legs and is lightweight and inexpensive. It can be placed on any stable surface and allows complete flexibility. Below are three models of tabletop stands: the first a decorative model, the second a folding design, and the third a concert style.

Cello Polish — Cellos require routine care. Using the correct polish is important to keep the instrument in good condition. Below are three of the many products available for you to use when caring for your cello. The kits include a cleaning agent and a polish.

Summary —This chapter showed some accessories that can help you play your cello more easily. To see more accessories for your cello, search "cello accessories," and you might spend the day looking through the results.

Chapter 5

How are Cellos Made?

Understanding how your cello is made helps you better understand how it works and how to play it. Cellos can be custom-made, handmade, or factory-made.

Custom-made means the cello and all its parts are made by a luthier (cello maker) for a certain customer. This is how it is done:

1. The luthier chooses the wood to be used. These may come from different parts of the world because the same kind of wood grown in different climates will grow differently.

    A. Maple wood is used for a cello's back, sides, and neck.

    B. Spruce wood is used to make the top of a cello.

    C. Ebony or rosewood are used for the fingerboard, pegs, purfling, and trim.

    Other kinds of wood and manmade products, such as plastic and metal, can be used as substitutes; however, maple, spruce, rosewood, and ebony are the best materials for making a good cello.

2. The next step is to design the instrument. Often, the luthier will begin by using a copy of the cellos of the great luthiers you will read about in chapter 6, such as Stradivari, Guarneri, and Amati. These models can then be adjusted to suit the plan for the new cello to be built.

3. When the wood and design patterns are decided upon, the luthier carves, shapes and molds the cello parts to fit the design selected.

4. The cello is assembled, stained, varnished, and hand-rubbed.

5. The luthier fits the instrument with pegs, a tailpiece, a bridge, and strings.

Handmade cellos can be made by more than one luthier within a shop. Each part of a cello is made by a maker who specializes in making that part. The handmade parts are assembled by another maker and set up by yet another. The instrument is still handmade but by more than one pair of hands.

Factory-made cellos are made of parts carved by computer-guided woodworking machines. The parts are put together by hand.

The Process

Step 1 – Making the Pattern — As explained in the custom-made section on the previous page, the luthier will decide on the size and shape of the cello. Usually, it will be a copy of one of the great masters such as Stradivari, Amati, or other master cello makers you will read about in chapter 6.

Step 2 – Selecting the Materials — The cello's major parts will be spruce for the top, maple for the sides, back, and neck, and ebony or rosewood for the fingerboard, pegs, and trim. Small inner parts called blocks and linings are often made of willow.

Definition: The "grain" is the shape or pattern of the fibers you see in a piece of wood.

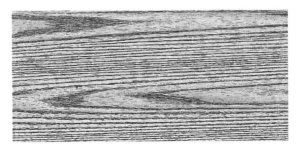

A cello made from wood with an even grain will produce a better sound than one with an uneven grain. If the luthier makes a one-piece top or back, the grain will spread out as it goes across the piece. If a triangle cut, which you will see on the next page, is used to make a two-piece top or back, the wood is taken from a smaller section of the tree, and the grain will be closer.

Step 3 – Cutting the Wood — There are two ways wood can be cut to make a cello's top and back (plates). For a two-piece top or back:

(A) A V-shaped block is cut out of a slice of a tree stump.

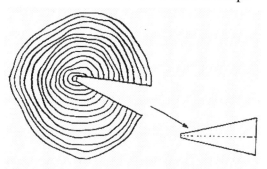

(B) The V-shape is cut down its center to form two separate triangular pieces.

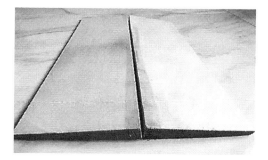

Step 4 – Joining the Cuts — The two pieces are joined together "book matched" with "hide glue," a glue that can be melted with warm water. The matched pieces of the two-piece top or back are placed to dry in a clamp. When dry, they will form one piece. Below are pictures of wood being "book matched," glued together, and drying in a clamp.

When the two pieces that have become one are removed from the clamp, an outline of a cello's back is traced onto that piece, and the wood is cut following the outline. The final result is a cello with a two-piece back, shown below.

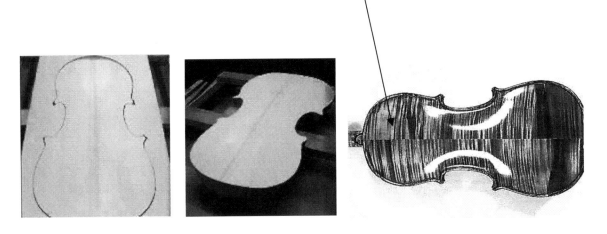

If the luthier decided on a one-piece back:

1. A layer of wood large enough to make an entire back or top is cut from a tree stump.

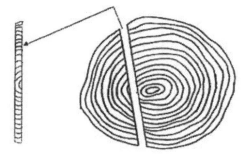

2. That wood slice is used to make a top or back without a seam in the middle.

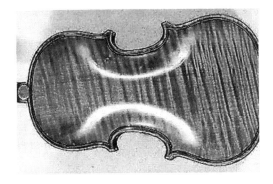

Definition: The term bout is used to identify the three sections of the cello's body. The upper third is called the upper bout, the middle section is called the C bout, and the lower third is called the lower bout.

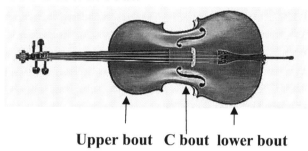

Upper bout   C bout   lower bout

Step 5 – The Mold — A mold is a cello-shaped wooden form that the luthier uses as a base for building the first parts of a cello.

The luthier will place six wooden blocks (arrows) on the mold to act as anchors for the instrument's sides or ribs. One (corner) block is placed in each of the four corners of the C bouts, and a fifth and sixth (end) block is placed at the mold's upper and lower end.

Step 6 – The Ribs — A cello's ribs (sides) are thin strips of maple wood. To create the ribs, the luthier wets thin wood strips to make them bend more easily. He or she then heats and bends the strips to shape and then glues them onto the six corner blocks shown here.

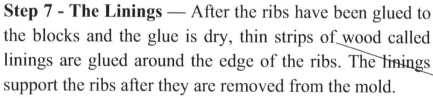

Step 7 - The Linings — After the ribs have been glued to the blocks and the glue is dry, thin strips of wood called linings are glued around the edge of the ribs. The linings support the ribs after they are removed from the mold.

Step 8 – Carving the Plates — In step 4, "joining the cuts," the top and back were rough cut. These must be carved into shapes that will produce the best possible sound.

Step 9 – Purfling — Purfling is a thin, double strip of wood that is set into the edge of the top and back of a cello. Purfling strengthens the edges of the cello and controls the vibrations traveling through the wood.

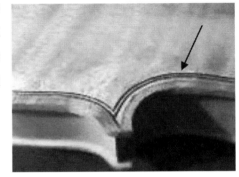

The pictures below show a luthier marking a groove (A), cutting a groove (B), and the finished product with the purfling installed (C).

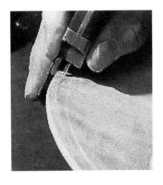

A   B   C

Step 10 – Tuning the Plates (Top and Back) — It is now time for the luthier to carve the wood of the cello's top and back plates so they will vibrate to produce the best sound for that instrument. There are two ways to decide how much and where wood should be removed from the two plates.

Originally it was done by the luthier tapping the plate and listening to the sound the tapping produces. Using the tapping method, the luthier gently holds a plate between the thumb and forefinger and, with the other hand, taps on the plate in different places. This will produce "tap tones," which are actual pitches showing the experienced luthier how much wood should be shaved from different plate areas to get the best sound.

In 1787 Ernest Chladni (pronounced Klad-nee), known as the father of acoustics (the study of sound), discovered that if you run a bow along the edge of a plate (cello top or back) held tightly in a clamp and sprinkled with glitter, the plate will vibrate. The glitter will move into certain patterns. The pattern of the glitter will show where vibration occurs and where to carve and not carve away some more wood. These patterns were called Chladni patterns. Below are two examples of Chladni patterns.

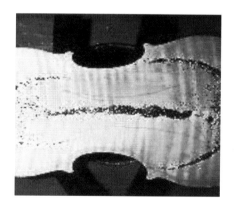 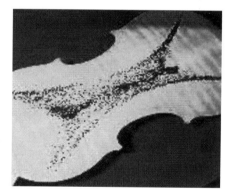

Step 11 – "f" Holes — The shape and size of the "f" holes or sound holes on a cello are an important part of the sound-producing system. A luthier can greatly improve a cello's sound by how the "f" holes are cut after the making process. "f" holes must be at least large enough to allow a sound post to pass through later in the making process.

To make the *"f"* holes, the luthier marks the shape on the cello's top plate and drills guide holes in places that will outline the pattern of the *"f"* hole. He or she then uses a jeweler's saw to make the cuts. The job is finished with a series of very sharp knives.

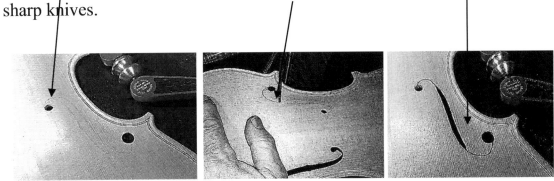

Step 12 - The Bass Bar — The bass bar is a strip of wood attached to the underside of the top plate. This strip strengthens the plate while spreading the lower pitches throughout the area.

The bass bar is glued and clamped in place.

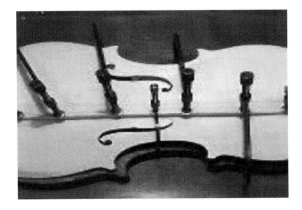

The clamps are removed when the glue is dry, and the luthier does another plate tuning, as described in step 10 above.

Step 13 – The Neck and Scroll — The neck and scroll are carved from one piece of hard wood (usually maple). The luthier draws an outline of the scroll on a wood block. He or she uses a hand saw, or electric saw to cut out the shape.

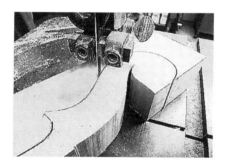 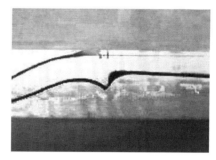

The location for the peg holes is marked on the cutout.

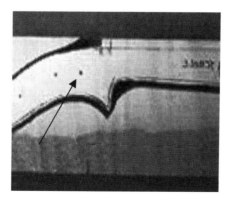

Step 14 – Peg Holes — Peg holes are drilled into the pegbox.

When those steps are completed, sharp knives and files are used to shape the neck.

 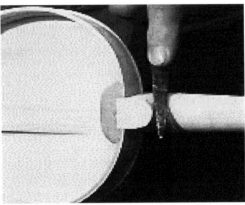

Step 15 – The Scroll — It is time to carve the scroll. The luthier does this using several different saws, scrapers, and carving knives.

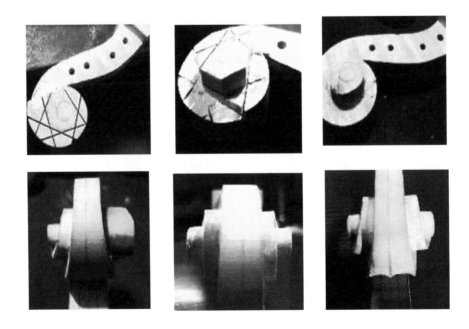

When those steps are completed, sharp knives and files are used to shape the pegbox.

Step 16 – Carving the Pegbox — The pegbox is the space for the pegs with wound strings. The pegbox sides (called cheeks) are marked on the wood block, and then the luthier uses a drill to start removing the wood.

Compliments of Hubert De Launay

Step 17— Finishing the Pegbox — When the extra wood is removed, the luthier switches to sharp carving tools such as chisels and gouges to carve out the remaining wood to form the pegbox shape and size.

This neck part is ready to be attached to the instrument's body.

Step 18 – Fitting the Neck to the Body — The neck must be perfectly in line with the cello's body so the strings will travel from the pegbox over the nut, fingerboard, and bridge to end at the tailpiece. A mortis (opening) is cut into the top block to fit the base of the neck, which is then glued in place.

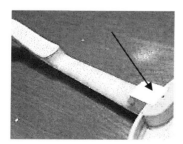 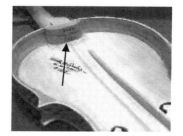

With the neck in place and the glue dry, the top and back plates are glued onto the ribs.

Step 19 — The Setup — A fingerboard is glued in place to complete the instrument before varnishing.

The nut and saddle are cut, finished, and glued in place.

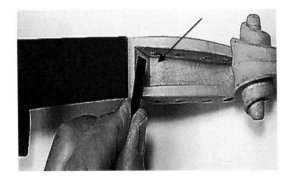 

Nut   **Saddle**

The pegs are shaved to fit the peg holes.

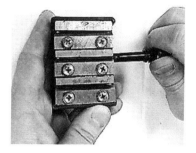

The peg holes are shaped and made larger (reamed).

The pegs are installed in the pegbox.

A bridge is cut to shape

The sound post is cut and put in place

An endpin, tailgut, and tailpiece are fitted and installed at the bottom of the instrument
.

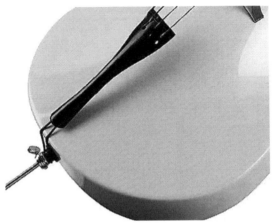

and the cello without a varnish finish is ready to be strung and tried for sound.

The cello has now been set up "in the white" (without a finish) for the first trial playing. At this time, the luthier will make any adjustments needed to improve the sound produced by this new cello.

Step 20 — **The Finish** — The coating put on the cello's raw wood after it is complete is called the "finish." The five steps used to finish a cello are:

(A) the preparation of the wood,

(B) putting on the first (ground) coat of wood treatment on the raw wood,

(C) coloring the wood,

(D) putting on a protective coating, and finally,

(E) polishing the cello.

A. Preparation — To prepare the raw wood, the luthier starts by wetting the wood surface to raise the grain. The wood is then sanded and scraped until the luthier is satisfied with the appearance of the raw (unfinished) wood.

B. Ground Coat — A ground coat is a liquid sealer that will prepare raw wood to receive color and a finishing product. The ground will fill the pores and cover any spots in the wood. The result will be a smooth surface on which to apply the next step in the finishing process.

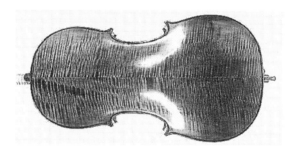

C. Color — The luthier chooses and applies color to the cello. He or she may wipe on the color with a cloth, spray it on, or brush it on.

D. Finishing Coat — The finishing coat will most often be varnish. Most luthiers agree that several coats of varnish with a fine sanding between each usually have the best result.

E. Polishing — When the varnish is dry, the luthier might improve the finish with hand polishing using any combination of oils, bees' wax, pumice, rottenstone, and turpentine.

Summary — And so, another handmade cello is born. With proper care, it can live for centuries. In the hands of professionals, it will provide the world with millions of notes that, when properly combined, will become music.

In the next chapter, you will read about the first person who plucked the string that made the sound that began the process that led to the cello. What a wonder. Thank you, luthiers, of the world, both past, and present, for your contributions to humankind's musical joy.

Chapter 6

What is the History of the Cello?

The first cello-like instruments began to appear in Italy in about the year 1525. Since the bow had not yet been invented, these string instruments were played by plucking or strumming the strings. Let's look at some of these "before-the-cello" instruments and see how they developed into the cello we now know.

Lesson One

Plucked Instruments

The Kantele — The Kantele is probably one of the earliest plucked instruments. It dates back several thousand years to the European countries that border the Baltic sea. The Kantele was used to accompany singing and was not a solo instrument.

The strings on the Kantele were stretched across the instrument's body, starting at the tuning pins and ending at a crossbar. Because there was no bridge or nut, the sound was more like a bell than a plucked string.

The strings were tuned to either a major or minor scale. The Kantele was placed on a flat surface or on the player's lap, where it could be strummed or plucked with the fingers or a guitar-like pick called a plectrum.

The "U" Shaped Lyre — The picture on the right is a "U" shaped lyre. Notice the shape of the instrument, starting from the two arms at the top that form a "U." Look at the body, and you will see the strings traveling over a bridge, passing a sound hole in place of the cello *"f"* hole on either side of the bridge, and the strings attached to a tailpiece.

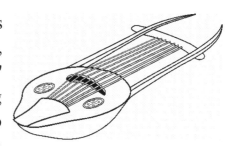

There is no fingerboard. The different pitches came from the thickness and tightness of the string. Look at your cello, and you will see the same idea. Your A string is the thinnest and, as such, the highest-pitched. Your D string is next in thickness and is lower-pitched than the A string. The G and C strings follow that pattern. As you can see by the shape of the lyre, it would be impossible to bow the strings. The strings had to be plucked.

The Lute — The lute begins to look something 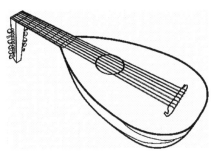 like a cello. At the top, it has tuning pegs attached to strings that travel over the nut. A big difference between the lute and the cello is in the finger-board's frets (metal strips), similar to those found on a guitar. Also, note that the strings are connected directly to the bridge instead of passing over a bridge, as do those on your cello.

Another difference between the lute and your 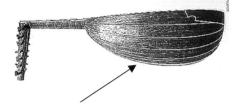 cello is the body's shape. The back of the lute body was made of strips of wood instead of one or two pieces of wood for the back of a cello.

The Zither — Zither is a name for string instruments with strings stretched across a soundboard. The zither is played on a flat surface or the player's lap.

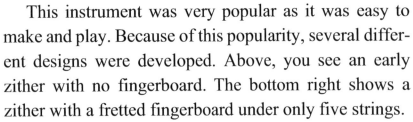

This instrument was very popular as it was easy to 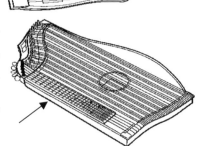 make and play. Because of this popularity, several different designs were developed. Above, you see an early zither with no fingerboard. The bottom right shows a zither with a fretted fingerboard under only five strings.

Timeline — Below is a timeline that shows some of the early plucked instruments as they might have appeared throughout history and the first appearance of a bowed instrument (bowed zither).

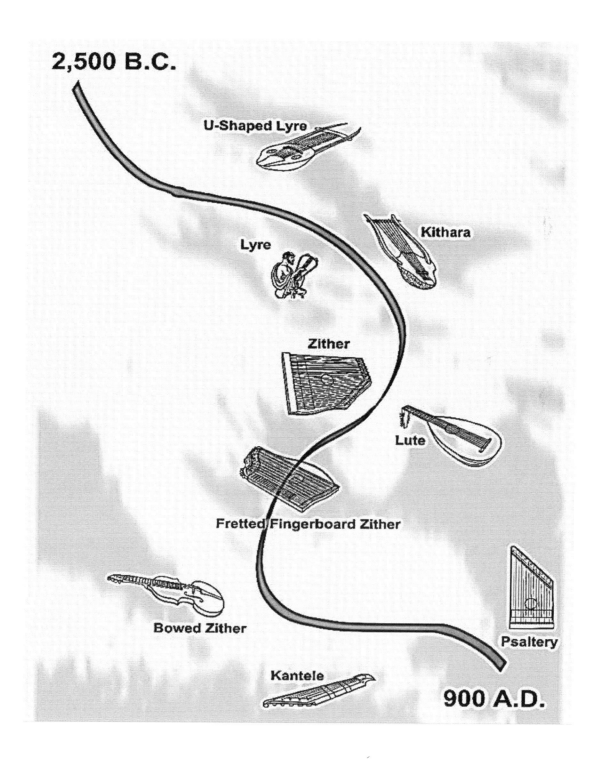

Lesson Two

Early Bowed Instruments

The Bowed Zither — The bowed zither arrives. Does it look familiar? Yes, we finally begin to see our cello shape appear. The zither has a body shape that will allow a bow to pass over the strings, **"ƒ"** holes on either side of the bridge, four pegs slightly different from those on your cello, and a fingerboard but with frets like a guitar.

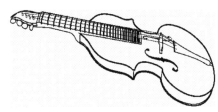

At some point in history, musicians began understanding that by rubbing a tacky stick or chord across a string, they were producing a richer sound than plucking the string. And so began the early but not yet cello-like bowed instruments.

In about 900 A.D., instruments with a body, fingerboard, pegbox, and tunable strings began to appear. Let's look at some of these instruments to see if we can find any more signs of a cello developing.

The Rebab — The rebab was an African bowed string instrument. The rebab was usually constructed with a pear-shaped body hollowed out from a block of wood. A thin sheet of wood or animal hide was attached to the hollowed-out section to act as a top. Unlike the modern cello, the fingerboard was part of the body instead of a separate piece attached to the instrument.

Rebabs usually had two or three strings that were played with a bow. As far back as the 8th century, the rebab was played in North Africa, the Middle East, and Europe.

The Spike Fiddle — Another form of rebab called a spike fiddle had a round body. The neck was a round pole supporting the strings and extended down through the body to form an endpin. The player held the spike fiddle upright, resting it on the ground as you do your cello.

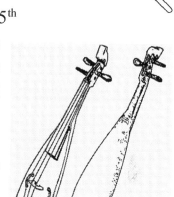

The Rebec — The rebec existed in Europe during the 15th and 16th centuries. The rebec is like a rebab except for the body. The body of the rebec was carved from a solid piece of wood. The body of the rebab was made from the dried shell of a plant. The shell was called a gourd.

We now begin to see the beginnings of a cello in the rebec. Up to now, most string instrument fingerboards were part of the instrument's body. Like the cello, the rebec's fingerboard was made separately and then attached to the instrument's body.

The Vielle — The vielle appeared in France during the Medieval period from the thirteenth to the fifteenth century. This instrument was closer in design to the modern cello. Rather than having a gourd-shaped body, as did the rebec, the vielle's body was constructed with a wider upper and lower section (bout) and a narrower midsection. This mid-section allowed a player to use a bow more easily.

The vielle had a flat pegbox with the pegs on top of the pegbox facing upward. The vielle had five strings.

Timeline — The timeline below shows the second phase in the development of string instruments.

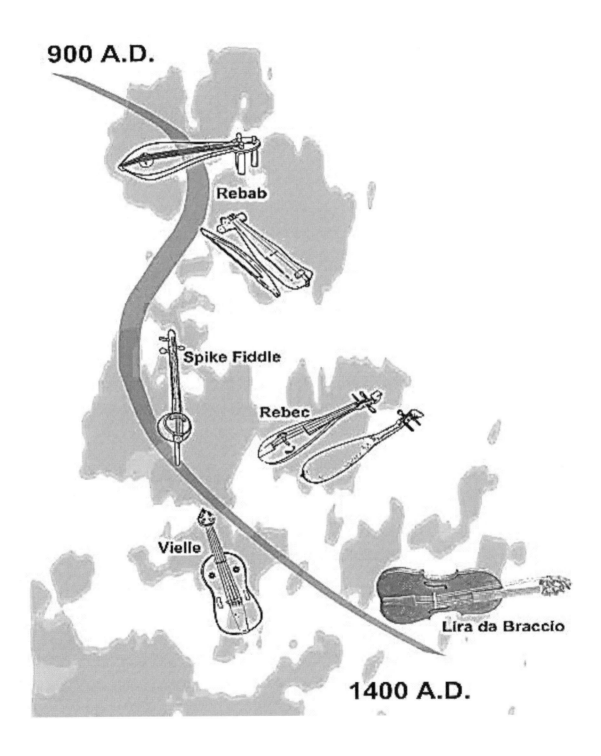

900 A.D.

Rebab

Spike Fiddle

Rebec

Vielle

Lira da Braccio

1400 A.D.

Lesson Three

Viols – The Birth of the Cello

The cello is often described as being a big violin. The cello came from the viol family of instruments that were similar to but definitely different from the violin. Viols were made in many different sizes, had frets like a guitar, and usually had six strings.

Below is a picture of a viol next to a violin. Notice the Viol has six strings and frets, whereas the violin has four strings and does not have frets. Also, note the difference in the sound holes. The viols are *"C"* shaped, whereas the violin sound holes are *"f"* shaped.

Viols enjoyed great popularity between the fifteenth and eighteenth centuries. These instruments were made in many different sizes to provide a complete range of notes. Smaller instruments played the higher notes, and as the instruments increased in size, they produced lower notes. At that time, performers began to favor a greater range of notes. To accommodate that need, instruments that played lower notes, such as your cello, began to be developed.

Because these instruments were of different sizes, they had to be held in different playing positions. Some were held under the chin with the arm as you would hold a violin or viola. Other larger ones were held on the lap, and still larger viols were held between the knees of the player. This being the case, the instruments took on the names of "Viola or Lira da Braccio" (of the arm) and "Viola da Gamba" (viola of the leg).

The Lira da Braccio (Lire of the Arm) — Following the vielle was the lira da braccio (Italian of the arm), which first appeared in Italy. This was a bowed string instrument resembling our present-day viola but with a wider fingerboard.

The Lira da braccio could have as many as seven strings. Four were tuned to E, A, D, and G over a fingerboard, as are those of a violin. Another low D string was placed over the fingerboard, and two other strings ran along the side of the fingerboard.

The tuning pegs on the lira da braccio were installed on the top of a leaf-shaped pegbox instead of on the sides as on your cello. The picture above shows a viola da braccio in the Kunsthistorisches Museum, Musikinstrumente, Vienna, Austria. This instrument was difficult to play because of the number of strings used to play melody and chords simultaneously.

Viola da Gamba (Viola of the Leg) — Below is a picture of a viola da gamba next to a modern cello. Note the similarities and differences. They look somewhat the same; however, a closer look will show the viola da Gamba with seven strings, a much wider fingerboard to accommodate the seven strings, frets on the fingerboard, different shaped sound holes, and no endpin.

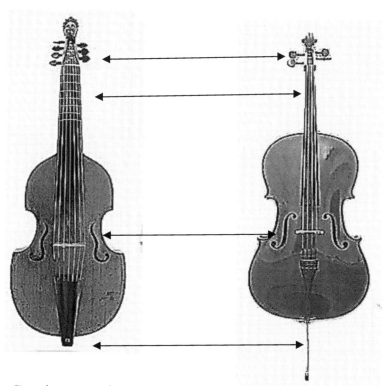

The Viola da Gamba was also made in different sizes to produce a wide range of notes. Eventually, seven different sizes of "Gambas" (short for Viola da Gamba) consisting of the highest-pitched called "pardessus," the treble "dessus," alto, and tenor "taille," a bass, and two different size contrabasses.

The Cello — We do not know exactly who made the first cello. At that time, luthiers began appearing in many different parts of Europe. It is believed that Gasparo da Salo of Brescia, Italy (C.1540-1609), and Andrea Amati of Cremona, Italy (C.1525-1611) were the two luthiers who probably made the first design for the cello that you now play. This cello evolved over about two centuries when it gradually took the place of the Viola da Gamba.

Pictured below is a cello made by Andrea Amati during the mid-sixteenth century that still exists and is in the National Music Museum in South Dakota. Note the artwork on the back of the instrument.

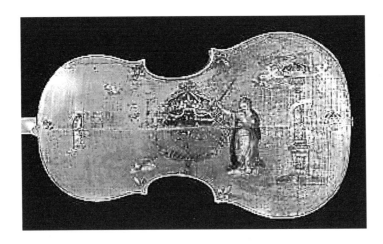

Lesson Four

The Schools

When you hear the word school, you will probably think of the building you go to for your cello lesson and to study other subjects. The word School can also have another meaning. A school can be where people interested in a subject, such as string instrument making, gather and live in a particular area to practice their art. Their goal is to develop their skills and broaden their knowledge of a subject.

The string instrument makers from the mid-fifteen hundreds to about 1725 gathered in "schools," where they developed and refined the cello to become the instrument we know and enjoy today.

Over some 200 years, such schools began to appear throughout Europe. The Brescian, Cremonese, Neapolitan, Tyrolean, and French schools were among them. Each is named for the geographic location where it was centered.

Timeline — Below is a timeline that shows the location of some of these "schools" in Europe and the luthiers who worked there.

(C.1784-1875)
Lupot, Vuillaume

(C.1620-1743)
Klotz, Stainer

Gasparo da Salo   *Amati, Bergonzi,*   Gagliano,*
Maggini, Rogeri   *Guarneri, Ruggieri, Stradivari*
(C.1585-1895)   *(C. 1541-1744)*

*Bergonzi & Gagliano worked in Cremona and Naples

Let's look into where some of the luthiers worked and what they did.

Cremonese School — Cremona Italy

Andrea Amati (1525-1611) was the principal figure in the Cremonese school of instrument making. His early works consisted of rebecs and other string instruments. His family consisted of Andrea, Antonio, Girolamo, Nicolo, and Girolamo II, all carrying on the Amati tradition of making extraordinary string instruments up to 1740. It is believed that Amati was the first luthier to make the forerunner to the cellos we know today. Many of the instruments they made are still being played.

Antonio Stradivari (1644 to 1737) was, and still is, the most famous violin, viola, and cello maker in history. In his mid-career, Antonio experimented with instrument sizes to develop a cello that became the prototype for other luthiers building the instrument. During his lifetime Stradivari made more than one thousand instruments.

Francesco Ruggieri (1620-1695) In addition to his work on violins and violas, Ruggieri is recognized for improving the design of the cello. Up to that time, cellos were much larger than the ones we know. Francesco reduced the size making the instrument more playable. His work became the basis on which today's cellos are made.

Carlo Bergonzi (1683-1747) was a neighbor and then a student of Stradivari. Bergonzi became Stradivari's repair technician.

Brescian School — Brescia, Italy

Brescia is the second-largest city in the Lombardy region of northern Italy, at the base of the Alps. Between 1585 and 1895, Brescia became a center for master luthiers. In Brescia, the Viol da braccio (of the arm), viol da gamba (of the leg), and the many other viols that had evolved up to that time became the models for today's cello. The luthiers of the Brescian school were considered to be among the best instrument makers. Unfortunately, an outbreak of a deadly disease spread throughout the region, killing most of the population.

Gasparo da Salo (1542-1609) — Gasparo developed an assortment of string instruments, including violones, a general term used for an assortment of larger string instruments. It is in this category that we would see the beginnings of early cello-like instruments. He also made other string instruments in the violin, viola, and double bass categories. Gasparo developed a longer-shaped violin which produced a more forceful sound. Gasparo was a double bass player of some note.

Giovanni Paolo Maggini (1580-1630) Maggini was a student of Gasparo da Salo. At about twenty years old, Maggini began developing his own cello designs with larger sound holes and a lower curving top. Maggini made about seventy-five instruments, mostly violins and violas, two cellos, and what might be one of the first double basses.

Neapolitan School — Naples Italy

In southern Italy, the area of Naples was growing. This growth increased the demand for musical instruments resulting in the development of the Neapolitan School of violin, viola, and cello making.

Alessandro Gagliano (1640-1725) — Alessandro Gagliano and his family made instruments for almost three hundred years up to 1925. Alessandro was the head of the family and is known for developing a brilliantly clear varnish with a beautiful red tint.

Tyrolean School — Mittenwald Germany

During that same period, the Tyrolean School grew where Jacob Stainer (1620-1683) and Matthias Klotz (1656-1743) were the most important luthiers.

Jacob Stainer (1620-1683) was one of the most important luthiers of his time. He developed a design for his instruments, which featured a higher arch on the top and back. He was also noted for his unique scrolls, which often featured carved heads instead of the traditional scroll shape.

Matthias Klotz (1656-1743) used his business skills to develop a complete string instrument industry. Like the Gagliano family, Klotz's business also became a family business, producing many instruments which are still available today.

French School — Mirecourt France

In 1635 there were 43 luthiers in Mirecourt, France. About a century and a half later, Nicholas Lupot (1784-1824) and Jean-Baptiste Vuillaume (1798-1875) were best known for producing excellent instruments based on the designs of previous masters. By the 20th century, Mirecourt had become the center of the violin, viola, and cello making business.

Nicholas Lupot (1784-1824) was most noted for copying the Stradivari design and designs of other masters. Nicholas did not distinguish himself so much for his originality but rather for the delicate refinement he added to the patterns of others.

Jean-Baptiste Vuillaume (1798-1875) was able to copy the styles and varnishes of the master luthiers of the past. In 1828 he started his own business where he sold his reproductions along with other high-quality instruments.

Summary — The "schools" of string instrument making mentioned above are only some of many that came into being throughout Europe beginning in the sixteenth century. Venice and Absam (Austria) schools and other lesser-known clusters of luthiers on every level developed the violin, viola, cello, and double bass that we enjoy today.

We cannot say exactly when and where the cello first appeared. The rebab, rebec, vielle, viola da gamba, and Viola da Braccio, along with all the experimental instruments that came and went over the centuries, paved the way for luthiers to settle on the violin, viola, cello, and double bass as the four instruments that satisfied the musical needs of performers. These instruments now provide a complete range of notes with timbres (tone quality) that are harmonious and complementary to one another and permit performers to play with great ease and musicianship. The references above are only an introduction to some of the luthiers of the time. A search on the internet will tell you much more about their work and lives.

Chapter 7

How Are Cello Bows Made?

Introduction — A cello bow looks like a stick with hair attached. It is made up of between thirteen and fifteen parts. The parts we see most easily are the stick, hair, and frog. Not easily seen are the hidden parts that keep the bow together.

As you read this chapter, have your bow handy and look at each bow part as it is discussed.

The Materials — The materials needed to make a bow are:

1. wood for the stick, often Pernambuco with a straight, dense grain
2. ebony for the frog
3. metal for the fittings
4. mother of pearl for the slide
5. hardwood plugs and wedges, and
6. a hank of horsehair.

The Stick — The first step in making a bow is choosing the wood to be used for the stick. The best bows are usually made with Pernambuco, a hardwood grown in Brazil. The bow maker (archetier) starts with a rectangular strip of wood called a straight blank the length of the bow. He or she then checks for defects in the grain, such as a knot or wormhole.

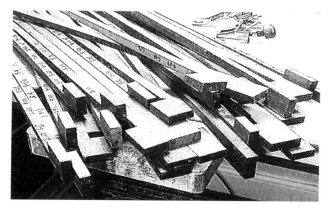

https://fiddlershop.com/blog/ Pernambuco-Cello-Bow-info

The blank is then roughly formed into a round or eight-sided (octagonal) shape.

The Head or Tip — After the stick is formed, the bow maker carves the tip of the bow.

When the tip is completed, a bone or ivory cover is glued in place, and a hole (mortise) is cut into its base to hold the tip end of the hair.

The Frog — The bow maker begins shaping a blank piece of ebony wood into a shape that is wider on the bottom than at the top. The sides of the wood are shaped to curve inward slightly.

He or she cuts a mortise into the frog in which the bow hair will be placed. Below is a frog with a mortise that is cut out and ready to accept hair.

The front of the frog will then be shaped into a "U," which faces the tip of the bow.

Below is a finished frog with the hair installed. The arrow points to a metal half-round band called a ferrule, which is placed over the end of the frog to hold the wooden wedge and hair in place.

On the underside of the frog behind the ferrule is a mother-of-pearl slide (A), which covers the mortise and holds the bow hair in place. Continuing from that slide is a silver plate (B) that travels up the back of the frog to its top. A mother-of-pearl eye (C) is placed on either side of the frog as a decoration.

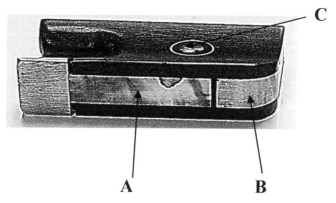

Fitting the Frog — The top of the frog is shaped to fit the stick. A metal strip called an underside is placed on the top of the frog to strengthen it, ease its sliding back and forth on the stick, and help support it and prevent cracking.

When finished, the frog is made up of a screw and an eyelet with a button on the end of the screw. The eyelet is screwed into the top of the frog. The screw goes into the eyelet, and the button is used to turn the screw.

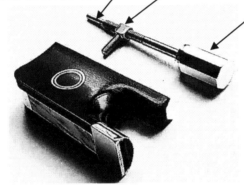

Creating a Curve (Camber) in a Bow Stick — To put the curve in a cello bow stick, the bow maker (archetier) heats the stick using a soft flame such as that from an alcohol lamp. When the stick has reached the proper temperature, it will begin to bend more easily. At that point, it is pressed against a form until it takes on the curve needed. The stick is then cooled and will keep the curved shape.

The Bow Grip — Just forward of the frog on the stick is a wrapping or bow grip which can be made of almost any material that can be wrapped around a stick. Most commonly used are whalebone, silver, leather, or rubber.

Completing the Stick — Let's review the work done thus far.

1. The archetier started with a "blank" strip of wood for the stick.

2. The stick was carved and shaped.

3. A frog was cut from a block of ebony wood.

4. A mortise was cut into the block to receive the bow hair.

5. The metal parts were added to the frog.

6. The tip of the stick was carved and shaped.

7. An ivory cover was glued onto the tip.

8. A mortise was cut into the tip to receive the bow hair.

9. The stick was heated and curved to create a proper camber (curve).

10. A grip was added to the stick just forward of the frog.

Hairing the Bow — The next step is hairing the bow. Use the diagram below, along with your own bow, as a guide while you read about the process.

To hair a bow, a hank of horsehair (A) is combed so that all hairs are parallel to one another. One end of the hank is then tied and forced securely into a box-shaped cutout (mortise) at the tip of the bow (B). The hair is held in place by a wooden, wedge-shaped plug (C) that is cut to exactly fit the space and hold the hair in place.

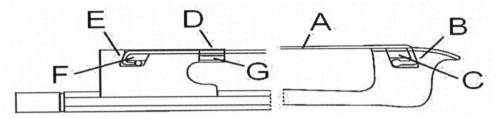

A ferrule (metal band) (D) is placed over the hair, which is stretched along the bow, tied at the other end, and set into a box-shaped cutout in the frog (E). A wooden wedge-shaped plug is placed into the box (F) to keep the hair in place. A slide and another wooden wedge are placed between the ferrule and the frog (G) to help distribute the hairs equally and keep them in place.

The archetier (bow maker) will make the stick's final adjustments to ensure it is straight, balanced, flexible, has the proper camber, and that the frog works properly. He or she will then color and polish the stick.

Summary — A bow is an important part of producing sound on a cello. For this reason, the quality of the hair and wood used, how the wood is formed into a well-balanced stick with proper camber (curve), and correct weight and balance are most important.

Chapter 8
What is the History of Bows?

The idea of making sound by rubbing something with a rough surface against a tight string might be how the very earliest bow came to be. Drawings dating back to the eighth-century show chords and hair tied or connected in different ways to bow-shaped sticks.

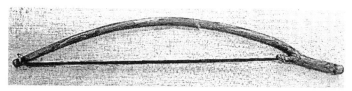

This arrangement would allow the chords or hairs to rub against a string, causing it to vibrate and produce a sound. Drawings of bows can be found in many different shapes. The one thing they all have in common is a curved stick that would hold a chord-like material or hair.

There is very little information on the early history of bows. Sculptures and paintings from the past hint at the cello's size, shape, structure, and playing positions, but those same works of art give little information about the bows. We might guess that the artists either did not know the important role bows had in sound production or that the bow was, in their minds, not important enough to deserve more detailed attention.

Beginning in the early 1600s, cello music changed from background rhythms to the melody. Playing rhythmic patterns required a simple bow that was short and had a wider arc, whereas to play the melody, musicians needed a more flexible, graceful overhand bow grip.

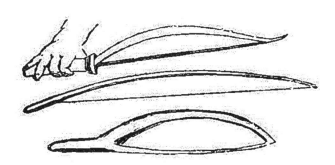

This hand position and a longer, better-balanced bow gave the player greater control. By using these newer designed bows, musicians produced various sounds ranging from very smooth and sensitive to crisp short separated notes. The bow sticks became straighter, lighter, and better balanced, and the frog that controlled the tension of the hair more refined.

The master archetier (bow maker), Eitan Hoffer, operates a shop in Israel where he makes bows for ancient instruments. Below are some pictures of Mr. Hoffer's bows which illustrate the shapes that came before the bows we now use.

The following examples of ancient bows were
reproduced with the permission of Eitan Hoffer

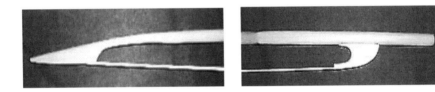

Renaissance Viol Bow Made from yew wood.

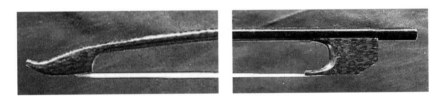

Short Viol Bow
Copy of an original Italian bow produced at the end of the 16th century.

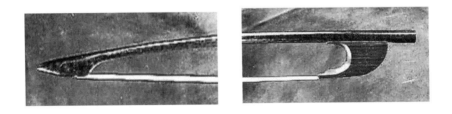

17ᵗʰ Century Style Bow
Made from snakewood, this bow is almost 26 inches long.

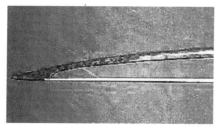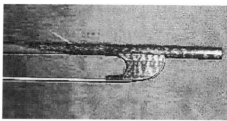

17ᵗʰ Century Short Bow
A reproduction of a bow from the year 1680. Look at
the difference in the size of the frog compared to the bow above.

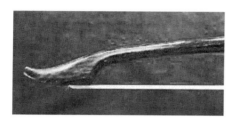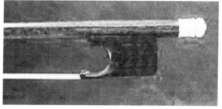

French 18th Century Bow with Screw Mechanism
This is an early snakewood bow with a movable frog.

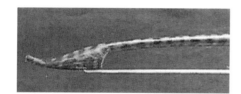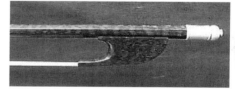

Viola "Long Sonata Bow" (c. 1720)
A copy of the original bow used for playing early 18ᵗʰ-century music
like that of J. S. Bach.

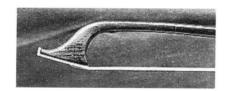

Classical Bow
Based on an original bow by N. Duchaine (c. 1765).

The Bow You Now Use

The bow you use to play your cello is an important part of the sound-making process. You use your bow to control the tone quality, clarity, volume, phrasing, and all the musical sounds you are making. You, your bow, and your cello are partners in the act of making music. Because of the importance of this three-way partnership, you must credit those bowmakers from the past who improved the ancient bows we saw above to develop the bow you now use.

François Xavier Tourte (1747-1835) had the greatest effect on developing the bow you use today. He was trained as a luthier by his father, Nicolas Pierre (1700-1765). François also began work on improving the bow. As he progressed, Tourte joined with G.B. Viotti, a violin virtuoso, in a successful effort to improve the design of the bow by changing the balance, increasing the weight of the frog and tip, and changing the bow's length. Tourte also refined the process for creating the camber (curve) in the bow stick by using heat instead of the carving method used at that time.

Added to that list of improvements, François invented the moveable frog using the screw and eye mechanism, which you now use to tighten or loosen your bow hair. He also developed a method to spread the hairs at the frog through a wedge of wood inserted between the hair and the ferrule. This small but very important addition resulted in the individual hairs being firmly held parallel to one another rather than clumping. (For a detailed view of these bow parts, see lesson 5 in Chapter 1).

An interesting story about François tells about his passion for perfection. François would destroy any bow made in his shop, which was not perfect in his judgment. The result was the possible loss of some great bows which, although not perfect enough in his eyes to enjoy life, would probably serve us as great tools. His bow design became the model for all the prominent bow makers to follow.

The three most famous bowmakers after Tourte were Ludwig Bausch (1805-1871), François Voirin (1833-1885), and Eugene Sartory (1871-1946).

Ludwig Christian August Bausch (1805-1871) followed Tourte as a maker of very fine bows. Ludwig lived and worked in Germany, where he and his two sons carried on the Tourte fine bow-making art until 1874.

François Nicolas Voirin (1833-1885) was a French maker of very fine bows. Many violists feel that these bows are the best made. Voirin redesigned the Tourte bow by thinning out the tip, changing the camber (curve) of the stick, and making it thinner at the heel (frog end).

Eugene Nicolas Sartory (1871-1946) was also a French maker of fine bows. His bows were made with stronger, thicker sticks and wider tips than the bows made by Voirin and Bausch.

Summary — At some point in the development of civilization, it was learned that rubbing a rough stick against a tight string would produce a sound. Ancient drawings and paintings which contain pictures of instruments and their bows show bow-shaped sticks with hair or chords connected to the stick on both ends. A musician could rub that chord or hair against a tight string and produce sound. From then on, people's creative ability took over to develop the bows you use to play your cello today. You will enjoy more information on their lives and achievements if you research each of the luthiers mentioned above.

NOTES

Chapter 9

A Dictionary for Cello Students

During your studies, you will come across unfamiliar words related to your cello or bow. This dictionary lists some of the words in alphabetical order and their meanings.

Terms Used for Bowing Directions

The universal language for music is Italian; however, other languages are also used.

Arco (Italian) — Use the bow to play this section.

Au Talon (French) — Play this passage at the frog end of the bow.

Avec le Bois (French) — Use the bow stick in place of the bow hair to bow the string.

Bow — An arch-shaped stick with a pointed tip on one end and a grip called a frog on the opposite end. Bows can be made of wood or manmade material. Horsehair or manufactured hair is stretched from the bow's tip to the frog, and the hair is drawn across a cello string to produce sound.

Brazilwood — A type of wood used to make bows.

Col Legno Battuto (Italian) — Strike the string with the wooden bow stick using a bouncing motion.

Collé (French) — Use a light short bow stroke. Attack from above using a brief contact with the string followed by a clean release upward.

Col Legno Tratto (Italian) — Use the bow stick in place of the bow hair to bow the string.

Détaché (French) — Bow detached notes smoothly with no pause between them.

Détaché Lance (French) — Bow detached notes smoothly with a slight pause between them.

Flautando (Italian) — Bow close to or slightly over the fingerboard's edge. Doing so will modify the sound to resemble a flute more closely. (See Sul Tasto below.)

Jeté (French) — "Throw" (bounce) the bow across the string to produce a series of short notes. Like skipping a rock across water.

Legato (Italian) — Use a smooth bowing motion with no break between notes except for the change in pitch.

Marcato (Italian) — Use a strong, bold bow stroke.

Martelé (French) — Use a strong accented attack to the note with immediate release.

Martellato (Italian) — Italian for Martelé. Use a strong accented attack to the note with immediate release.

Pernambuco — A wood grown in South America. This wood is considered to be the finest for making bows.

Pizzicato (Italian) — Pluck the string.

Ponticello (Italian) — Direct the bowing close to the bridge to produce a stronger sound. See Sul Ponticello below.

Punta d'arco (Italian) — Direct the bowing to the tip of the bow to produce a softer sound.

Ricochet (French) — Bounce the bow off the string in a series of notes.

Sautillé (French) — Use a light bow stroke bouncing across the string.

Spiccato (Italian) — Use a bouncing bow stroke across the string to produce very short-separated notes

Staccato (Italian) — Produce a short note using any of the "separated note" techniques listed.

Sul (Italian) — Sul means "on." It also indicates "near" as in "sul pointicello."

Sul Pointicello (Italian) — Bow near the bridge to produce a stronger sound.

Tasto (Italian) — The fingerboard.

Sul Tasto (Italian) — Bow over or near the fingerboard to produce a softer sound.

Tremolo (Italian) — Play the same note repeatedly by moving the bow back and forth rapidly with a wrist motion.

Trill — Fast back-and-forth changing of two notes a half or whole step apart.

Vibrato (Italian) — A repeated fast slight change in pitch.

NOTES

Chapter 10

A Review of Cello Parts

Back — The back of the body of a cello, also called the backplate.

Bass Bar — A strip of wood on the underside of the top of a cello, reinforcing the top and distributing the lower notes throughout the top.

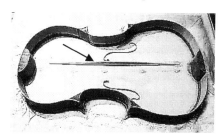

Belly — The top of a cello, sometimes called the top plate.

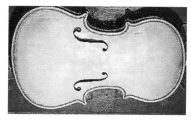

Bridge — A support for the strings on a cello. The bridge transfers sound from a vibrating string to the instrument's top.

Bow — A curved stick made of wood or a manmade substance strung with horsehair or a fiberglass hair substitute. When used, the ribbon of hair is drawn across the strings of a cello to produce sound.

Bow Hair — Horsehair or a manmade substitute strung across a bow.

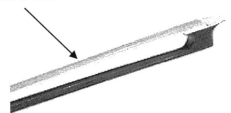

Body — The main part of a cello. The body (front, back, and sides) strengthens the sound produced by the vibrating strings.

Block — A wooden block placed at key points in the body of a cello to strengthen the unit. One block is placed in each corner where the upper and lower bouts (see below) meet the C bout. One block is placed at the bottom of the body to reinforce the endpin and one at the top to reinforce the neck contact.

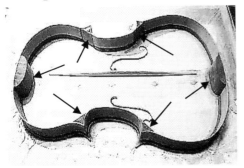

Bout — The word used to identify the three sections of a cello body. The upper third is called the upper bout, the middle section is called the C bout, and the lower third is called the lower bout.

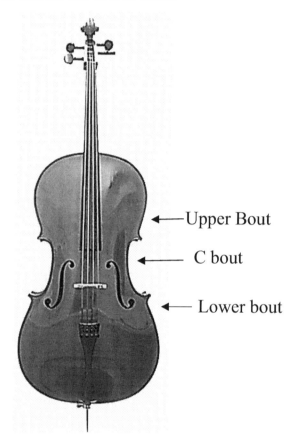

←—Upper Bout

←— C bout

←— Lower bout

Endpin — The adjustable metal rod at the bottom of a cello. The endpin rests on the floor to support the cello.

"f" Hole —Sometimes called a sound hole, an *"f"* hole is an *"f"* shaped opening in the top of a cello, which allows the sound vibrations to escape from the instrument.

Fine Tuner — A device on a string or tailpiece that, when turned, will slightly adjust the pitch of a string.

Fingerboard — A hardwood board (usually ebony) that extends from the pegbox to provide a surface against which you can press the string to change pitches.

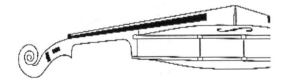

Lining — Thin strips of wood glued around the inside edge of the ribs of a cello to strengthen it.

Mutes — A mute changes the tone, quality, and volume of a cello's sound. Mutes can be made of wood with three prongs, a rubber disc, wire with a plastic arch, or five rubber prongs. Below are four examples of mutes for a cello.

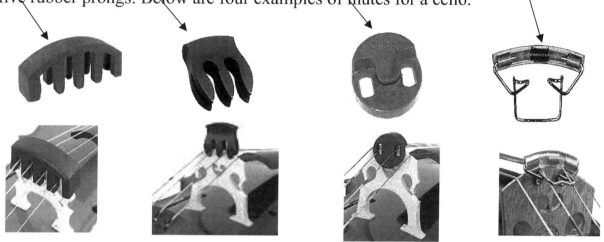

Nut — The wooden insert over which the strings pass from the pegbox to the fingerboard.

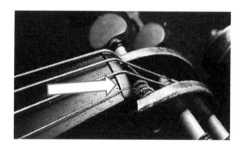

Peg — A wedge-shaped (smaller on one end than the other) piece of wood to which cello strings are connected to tune them.

Purfling — Two parallel strips of hard wood, usually ebony, are inlaid into the edge of the top and back of a cello to strengthen the edges and control vibration.

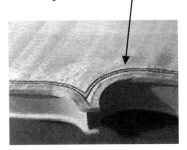

Ribs — The sides of a cello.

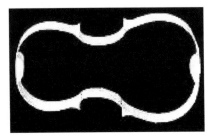

Saddle — A hardwood bar placed at the end of the top of a cello to support the tailgut and prevent damage to the body.

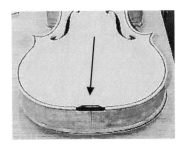

Sound Post — A wooden dowel (post) that supports the top of a cello and conducts the vibrations produced by the higher strings from the top of the cello to its back.

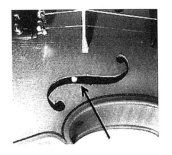

Scroll — The decorative top of a cello.

Scroll Eye — The center of a scroll.

Tailpiece — A device to which the lower end of cello strings are attached. Some tailpieces have fine tuners built into them.

Tailgut — A short piece of gut or nylon that secures the tailpiece to the end pin.

Wolf Tone Eliminator — Eliminates the wobbling tone that sometimes happens, usually on the G# on some cellos.

Index